PAKISTAN AND BANGLADESH

BY EMIL LENGYEL
PAKISTAN AND
BANGLADESH

REVISED EDITION | FRANKLIN WATTS, INC. | NEW YORK, 1975

Photographs courtesy of Pakistan Mission to the United Nations, with exception of page 40, courtesy Charles Phelps Cushing.

Library of Congress Cataloging in Publication Data

Lengyel, Emil, 1895–
    Pakistan and Bangladesh.

    (A First book)
    First ed. published in 1972 under title:
Pakistan.
    Bibliography: p.
    Includes index.
    SUMMARY: Introduces the history, geography, economy, government, culture, and people of Bangladesh and Pakistan emphasizing the differences between them.
    1. Pakistan — Juvenile literature. 2. Bangladesh — Juvenile literature. [1. Pakistan. 2. Bangladesh] I. Title.
DS376.9.L45   1975   954.9   75-8996
ISBN 0-531-00762-6

CONTENTS

ALSO BY THE AUTHOR:

Asoka the Great
Lajos Kossuth
Jawaharlal Nehru
Ignace Paderewski
Turkey
Iran
Modern Egypt
The Oil Countries of the Middle East
Siberia
The Colony of Pennsylvania
The Colony of New Hampshire

PAKISTAN AND BANGLADESH

CHAPTER ONE
A SPLIT IN THE ISLAMIC REPUBLIC

In December, 1971, the former eastern wing of the Islamic Republic of Pakistan declared itself to be the new country of Bangladesh. (The name means "Bengal Nation.") This action was the result of long-standing conflict between what had been Pakistan's two sections and of a short, bitter war between India and Pakistan.

When Bangladesh declared its independence, Pakistan said that it wanted some sort of union between the two areas. Just as it took time for this crisis to develop, it may take a good deal of time for Pakistan and Bangladesh to solve their problems.

How did this crisis come about? How did a young country find itself so bitterly torn apart? To understand what happened in December, 1971, we must try to understand the nation that was established in 1947 as the Islamic Republic of Pakistan. (To distinguish between the country before and after December, 1971, we shall call it the Islamic Republic when referring to the time before the split.)

One major country in the world included the main religion of its people in its name. It was the Islamic Republic of Pakistan. Islam is the religion of more than 500 million people. Over 130 million of them lived in the Islamic Republic. The word *Islam* means "submission" — to God, Allah. The word *pakistan* means "land of the pure" in Urdu, now the national language of Pakistan.

The Islamic Republic's neighbor was the Republic of India. The bulk of India's population — some 570 million — are Hindus. They do not "submit" to one God, as do the followers of Islam, known as Muslims. Some Hindus believe that there are forty *crores* of gods. *Crore* is an Indian word meaning 10 million. Forty crores, therefore, means 400 million — a huge collection indeed.

The Islamic Republic and India became independent in 1947. Even though they were new as independent nations, they were ancient lands. Until independence, they formed the most important part of the British Empire, on a vast peninsula of Asia so large that it is called a subcontinent. Under the British, it was known as the Indian subcontinent.

Even after the British left, the Indians wanted to continue the unity of the subcontinent. But the Muslims wanted a country of their own, on the grounds that Islam and Hinduism are not only two different religions but two different ways of life. What is permissible for the Muslim, for instance, is frequently not permissible for the Hindu. Eating beef is allowed the Muslim, forbidden to the Hindu. Drinks that are allowed the Hindus are forbidden to the Muslims. Episodes in Indian history, of which Muslims are proud, may be the causes of shame to the Hindus. Even though the Hindus have always been in a majority on the subcontinent, the rulers of the best parts of it were Muslims.

The social life of the Hindus, too, is entirely different from that of the Muslims. Tradition-minded Hindus have a rigid caste system. To the Muslim all people are supposed to be equal. Family life is also different. Great occasions — weddings and births — are celebrated differently, and funeral ceremonies vary. The ideas of the two religions concerning life after death are far apart. Days of rejoicing for the Muslims may be days of sorrow for the Hindus. The lives of women, the place of the teacher, are different in the two communities. Their social structures as a whole have little in common.

Because of the differences, feuds between the Hindus and Muslims were frequent under the British rule, and even before. These were the so-called communal strifes. In spite of them the two communities lived side by side. Yet they did not live "together," since there was little social contact between them. That is why the Muslims insisted on the parting of the ways that led to the establishment of the Islamic Republic of Pakistan.

Even before independence, the Muslims had two compact places of settlement, one in the northwest and the other in the northeast. Therefore the country was established with two wings (zones or provinces), containing the bulk of the Muslim population on the subcontinent. The wings were separated by nearly one thousand miles. India was in between the two zones. Still, additional millions of Muslims lived in settled areas in India. And millions of Hindus lived in the Islamic Republic.

One might have expected the two wings to be alike in their ways of life, social structures, occupations, perhaps even climate. Curiously, perhaps no two parts of the world were more different than were the two zones — in geography, rainfall, customs, characteristics, or complete ways of life. They spoke different languages — mainly Urdu in the west, Bengali in the east; ate different foods — meat and wheat in the west, rice and fish in the east; and belonged to different parts of the world — the west to the Middle East, the east to Southeast Asia.

These differences eventually led to the split into two countries. But before 1971, the only bond that united the two zones was their common religion, which is the reason the country was called the Islamic Republic.

CHAPTER TWO
THE GEOGRAPHY

Pakistan, more than five times the size of Bangladesh, has a population nearing 70 million. Bangladesh contains more than 75 million people. The reason Bangladesh has more people is that Pakistan is partly arid, while Bangladesh is literally soaked in rain. Because there is abundant rain, more crops can be grown and more people can be fed.

Pakistan covers some 310,000 square miles, slightly smaller than the combined states of California, Oregon, and Washington. Bangladesh has about 55,000 square miles, making it about one-third the size of California.

In the north, at "the top of the world," Pakistan leans against the highest mountains on earth, in the Karakorum Range. The Godwin Austen peak, more correctly called K2, is the world's second highest mountain, next to Mount Everest. It is 28,250 feet high. (Everest rises to 29,028 feet.) Some sixty peaks, forming a huge arc that shields the subcontinent in the north, are more than 24,000 feet high.

Pakistan is flanked by Iran and Afghanistan to the west and northwest. Only the narrow Afghanistan panhandle separates it from the USSR in the north. To the east are Kashmir and India. (Pakistan and India have a yet unsolved dispute over Kashmir.) To the south is the Arabian Sea. From the "top of the world" to the Arabian Sea, the straight-line distance is about one thousand miles.

Bangladesh is surrounded by India to the west, north, and east, except for a short border with Burma in the southeast. Directly south is the Bay of Bengal.

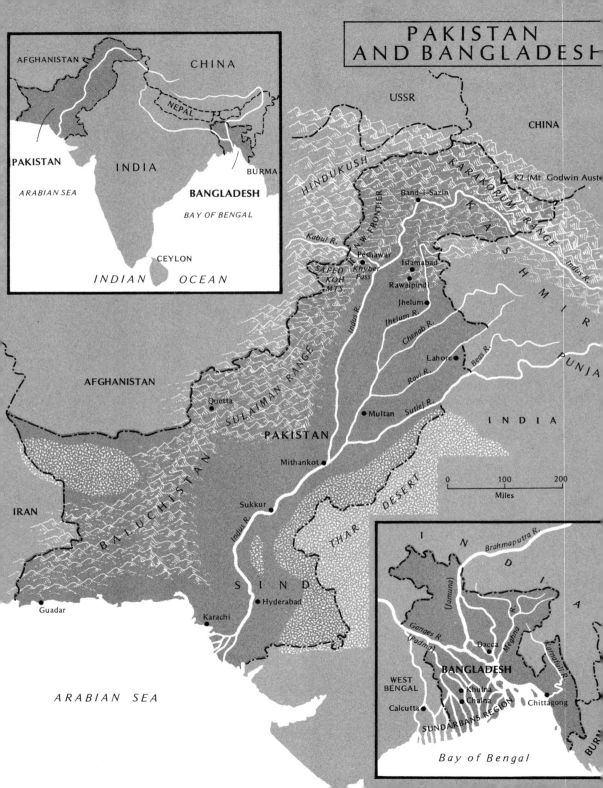

PAKISTAN
AND BANGLADESH

Inset map (upper left):

AFGHANISTAN

CHINA

NEPAL

PAKISTAN

INDIA

ARABIAN SEA

BURMA

BANGLADESH

BAY OF BENGAL

CEYLON

INDIAN OCEAN

Main map:

USSR

CHINA

HINDUKUSH

KARAKORUM RANGE

K2 (Mt. Godwin Aust

Band-i-Sazin

N.W. FRONTIER

Kabul R.

Peshawar

Khyber Pass

Islamabad

Rawalpindi

SAFED KOH MTS.

Jhelum

Jhelum R.

Indus R.

Chenob R.

K A S H M I R

Lahore

Beas R.

Ravi R.

PUNJA

Sutlej R.

Multan

INDIA

AFGHANISTAN

Quetta

SULAIMAN RANGE

PAKISTAN

Mithankot

0   100   200
Miles

THAR DESERT

Sukkur

Indus R.

IRAN

BALUCHISTAN

S I N D

Hyderabad

Guadar

Karachi

ARABIAN SEA

Inset map (lower right):

I   N   D

Brahmaputra R.

(Jamuna)

R.

Ganges R.

Dacca

Megna

(Padma)

BANGLADESH

Karnafuli R.

WEST BENGAL

Khulna
Chalna

Chittagong

Calcutta

SUNDARBANS REGION

BURM

Bay of Bengal

CHAPTER THREE
PAKISTAN

The Indus River has given its name to many parts of the world — to India and the Indian subcontinent, to the West Indies (largely because Columbus thought he had reached India), and also to the American Indians.

As it rushes down from the top of the world, the Indus swirls around the Nanga Parbat, the 26,660-foot peak in northwest Kashmir. From an elevation of 13,000 feet, the river hurtles down to lower-lying plains, absorbing the waters of the other glacier-fed streams.

THE PUNJAB

The nearly 2,000-mile-long Indus River enters Pakistan in the north at Band-i-Sazin. Farther down it is joined by the waters of five tributaries, which give the name to this most important part of the country. It is called the Punjab, meaning "five rivers." (Since independence, the Punjab is divided into east and west, the West Punjab belonging to Pakistan.) The tributaries are the Jhelum, Chenab, Sutlej, Beas, and Ravi.

The Punjab is the breadbasket, or wheat country, of Pakistan. By international agreement, Pakistan uses the waters of the two western-most streams — the Jhelum and Chenab — together with those of the Indus. These waters are harnessed in dams. The Pakistani describe Tarbela Dam in the northwest as the greatest in that part of the world.

When the Indus strikes out on its southward slope near the dam, it begins to share some of the traits of Egypt's Nile River. The climate becomes drier, the rain scantier, the soil thirstier. There are farmlands only where there are canals. Farther south, where the soil is rocky and pebbly, the Indus flows between desolate banks. It finally reaches the Arabian Sea south of Karachi, not far from the Indian border.

Except for Karachi, Pakistan's largest cities are located in the Punjab. "One can see nothing more beautiful in the seven regions of the world," sang the seventeenth-century poet Talib Amuli about the city of Lahore, in the northeastern part of the province. Zam-Zama, "the lion's roar," is the name of the old cannon resting on a brick platform in front of the Wonder House Museum. It is said that whatever power is in possession of the cannon will also be in possession of Lahore, Pakistan's cultural center and most historic city.

The Shalimar Gardens of Lahore have been spoken of as the most beautiful landscape architecture in the world. Although the gardens have deteriorated now, they cover some eighty acres and were built on three terraces in the seventeenth century, by order of Shah Jahan. The profusely decorated marble tomb of Shah Jahangir was also ordered by Jahan to honor his father.

The Great Mosque (Bahshahi Madjid) of Lahore is said to have the largest open courtyard for worship in the world. It holds sixty thousand people. The huge gold-tipped domes of this seventeenth-century structure can be seen for miles. Lahore is also the site of the Pearl and Golden mosques. Its sixteenth-century fort and imperial residence recall that the city was the home of some of the greatest rulers of the land, including Akbar the Great.

The bazaar of Lahore is a colorful, busy, and noisy place. Its narrow lanes resound with hammering craftsmen's tools. The men work, talk, sing, and quarrel all day long in its lanes, each reserved for a craft — pottery, metalware, leather goods, and others. The alleys also echo with the bargaining of buyers and sellers. These transactions are supposed to be for the purpose of settling on a price, but often they are also appreciated as displays of sharp wit.

Left: central terrace
of the Shalimar Gardens.
Right: Pakistan Provincial
Assembly Building at Lahore.

Lahore has grown a good deal since the country gained independence in 1947. The flood of refugees from India descended mainly on the cities, where job opportunities seemed to be greatest. Lahore now has a population of nearly two million.

Rawalpindi in the north is usually known as Pindi. Once the largest military station in British India, it served as the Islamic Republic's national capital from 1959 to 1967. A modern-looking city, it is an important grain market. European churches, the fort, the arsenal, and the "English" public park are all evidences of its past.

The city of Islam — Islamabad — is only a twenty-minute drive north from Pindi. It became the national capital of the Islamic Republic in 1967, after six years of building, and is now Pakistan's capital. As does the name of the country, the name of the capital stresses the uniqueness of Pakistan, a nation dedicated to Islam.

Islamabad is situated on a tableland, over an area of 350 square miles, within view of the Murree Hills, a popular summer resort. Surrounding it is an expanse of natural terraces and meadows, rising to 2,000 feet above sea level.

The city itself is divided into zones. The administrative zone (or sector), situated on the main axis of the capital, contains the president's house, assembly buildings, the supreme court, ministries, and eight massive, multistoried secretariat blocks for government offices. A special zone of five hundred acres has been provided for foreign diplomatic missions, close to the picturesque Lake Rawal. A small stream meanders through this area.

The residential sectors have been set up in rows on both sides of the center, in the heart of Islamabad. Each residential zone is a self-sufficient township, with civic facilities, such as schools, mosques, dispensaries, markets, and parks. A vast valley has been earmarked for a national park, with institutions of countrywide importance, such as an Olympic village, a national health center, an atomic research institute, and exhibition grounds. The Grand National Mosque, outdoing even Lahore's Great Mosque, can hold some 100,000 people, a record number for a Muslim shrine.

THE NORTH-WEST FRONTIER

The North-West Frontier province of Pakistan is only one-fourth the size of Punjab and has one sixth of its population — more than 10 million. Yet it is probably the better known of the two regions. This is because it is located near the eastern entrance of the Khyber Pass, a zigzagging, narrow, twenty-eight-mile-long cut through the Safed Koh Mountains of the Hindu Kush region, which links northwestern Pakistan with Afghanistan. The mountains look stark, angular, rugged, and dusty. More forbidding are the guardhouses and forts at strategic turns. And still more forbidding are some of the armed men who stand guard there. Much of the import trade of Afghanistan, which has no natural access to the sea, must travel through the pass.

A plaque at the entrance of the pass is entitled "The Legend of the Khyber Pass." It says: "The North-West Frontier of Pakistan has seen, perhaps, more invasions in the course of history than any other country in Asia and, indeed, in the world."

The number of invaders who have crossed this pass is staggering indeed. The Khyber Pass links the Indian subcontinent with the rest of Asia. For countless generations, India was a magnet that attracted would-be conquerors from less-advantaged regions.

Because of its rugged looks, its warlike people, and its role as the shield of India, this region has been the scene of numerous motion pictures and novels.

Peshawar, the "big city" of the frontier, is only a few miles from the Khyber Pass. Its "Street of the Story Tellers" tells a tale of its own. There stories have been told from all parts of Asia to those ready for rest after dangerous trips across the great mountains. Peshawar used to be a meeting place for large numbers of merchants from across the Himalaya, Karakorum, and Hindu Kush ranges.

The North-West Frontier is also the home of the Pathans, who speak their own language, called Pashto. When India was ruled by the British, these frontiersmen waged *jihads* — sacred wars — against the British Empire.

Now the Pathans are citizens of Pakistan. But the national gov-

Victoria Road,
one of the main streets
in Karachi

ernment rules them in only a limited way. They live under their own kings or chieftains, called *maliks*. The chieftains remain in power only so long as they remain strong. They are aided by the *jirgas,* or tribal councils.

Honor — *izzat* — is the guiding word for the Pathans. They are very sensitive people, and the slightest insult may call for bloodshed. As a result, feuds are numerous and endless.

The traditional greeting in the Muslim world is *Salem aleykum* — "peace with you." The traditional farewell is *Kuda hafiz* — "May the Almighty save you." But the Pathans are different in this respect, too. Their welcome means "Don't get tired!" Obviously, getting tired may be dangerous in this part of the country. Their farewell means "Don't get old!" The old cannot defend their honor as well as can the young and strong.

THE SIND

The name of the southern province of Sind (shortened from *sindhi*) means "collection of water." This area contains about 15 million people.

Much of the region is desert. *Thar* ("salt") is the name of the desert that India shares with Pakistan. The farther south one goes, the less is the rainfall, and only irrigation keeps farming at a possible level. Even the few cultivated areas are often covered with a film of fine sand.

Karachi, Pakistan's largest city and the national capital from 1947 to 1959, is located in the Sind. During World War II, this port on the Arabian Sea had a population of 360,000. Today its people number more than 3½ million, many of them refugees living in unbelievable squalor. Karachi has grown faster than any other large city in the country.

There is little to see in the outlying areas around Karachi. It is surrounded by a desolate area of sunbaked hills on one side and by swamps and deserts on the others. The city has the only functional harbor in Pakistan and is, therefore, very important. It was also an important port under the British.

With the creation of the Islamic Republic in 1947, Karachi became the first capital of the new country. All new government buildings had to be hurriedly built. More than other Pakistani cities, Karachi attracted refugees, because of the new capital's need for workers.

Due to its location, Karachi developed into the most important industrial area in the country. Indeed, as much as about half of the industry in Pakistan is located there. Mainly these plants turn wheat into flour, cotton into textiles, sugarcane into sugar, and minerals into chemical and pharmaceutical products.

Unfortunately, Karachi grew too fast, and now it suffers from all the ills of large cities. Still worse, it also has a trying climate, which may often soar far above 100 degrees Fahrenheit, and that did not stimulate government efficiency. So it was decided to transfer the capital into the hill country of the north. Some Sindhis feel exploited by the Punjabis. "Long live Sind" is the slogan of their independence movement — a movement that has not progressed very far as yet.

BALUCHISTAN

This province is located in the extreme southwest, bordering on Iran and Afghanistan. Baluchistan has a larger area than that of the Punjab but only a tiny fraction of its population — less than 2 million. It is one of Pakistan's most sparsely populated zones.

Only one acre in ten is fit for cultivation in this region. The province produces about one percent of the total wheat production in Pakistan, and grows practically no sugarcane or cotton, the main staples of its neighboring provinces. The industrial production of Baluchistan counts for only one half of one percent of the country. Many of the people are herders.

The scant vegetation in this province is found on its higher spots, where the summer temperatures are less cruel and where passing clouds sometimes bring sporadic rains.

Quetta, the main city of the province, is very pleasant, located in the cooler atmosphere of a high plateau. It is not only a business and military center but also a transportation and trade hub.

THE CLIMATE

The subcontinent runs to extremes in so many ways that it should not be surprising to learn that its climate is extreme, too.

Pakistan has greater extremes of temperature than does Bangladesh, but it is much drier. The annual rainfall varies from under five inches in the Sind to about forty inches in some parts of the Punjab. During the summer months, daily average temperatures on the plains may reach 90 degrees, and readings of over 100 are common. In the cooler months, November to March, the temperature on the plains may drop as low as 55 degrees, and sometimes heavy snow falls in the mountains west of the Indus River.

Some parts of southern Pakistan are among the hottest places in the world. The noted British historian Arnold Toynbee once told a story of waiting for a train in the Baluchistan city of Sibi. The temperature at noon was 129 degrees in the shade. But Toynbee's Pakistani companion consoled him by saying that they would be in Karachi by evening, fanned by gentle breezes from the sea. When they reached Karachi, the temperature was 100 degrees and the humidity 100 percent.

In a climate such as this, heatstrokes are common and hard work is especially tedious. People simply must slow down.

CHAPTER FOUR

BANGLADESH

Several huge rivers are the mixed blessing of Bangladesh. Much of Pakistan is arid; all of Bangladesh is rich farmland, rain forest, and swamp. All of Pakistan is in the southernmost temperate zone; all of Bangladesh is in the tropical and subtropical regions.

Pakistan has four provinces; Bangladesh has one — Bengal. Adjacent India has its own Bengal state. To distinguish between the two, Bangladesh's share has been called East Bengal. West Bengal, in India, contains the largest city on the subcontinent, Calcutta, which has a population nearing 8 million.

DACCA

The largest city in Bangladesh is its capital of Dacca in the south-central part of the country. The population rose from some 80,000 about twenty-five years ago to over one million today. Much of the increase was due to the partition of India and the Islamic Republic. Dacca has a large percentage of refugees from India.

If religious devotion can be measured by the number of places of worship, Dacca must be one of the most religious cities in the world. It is said to have some seven hundred mosques.

At one time Dacca was the capital of all Bengal. Its fort, which its rulers never completed, was to be named Lal-Bagh — "beautiful garden." The city was once famous for the muslin it produced, a soft, thin, fine, handwoven cloth for women's garments. Dacca also has a rich tradition in turning out silver filigree and shell bracelets. A few of its bazaar craftsmen still produce mother-of-pearl buttons, carved shells, horn combs, and delicate articles of silver and gold. Dacca has jute-pressing plants and shipyards. Boats are a most important means of transportation in this soaking-wet land. City plants also produce electric supplies and chemicals.

Dacca is called Little Calcutta, after the sprawling metropolis of West Bengal. Like its namesake, Dacca is plagued by countless problems, partly due to the influx of refugees and partly because of poor administration. For instance, with all the water available, little of it is safe to drink in the city. Unemployment is out of hand and the number of beggars is large.

The Daccans and Bengalis are articulate. What is on their minds is soon on their lips. Demonstrations are everyday events for all kinds of causes. The beggars, following the local custom, have also presented their demands: no offering can be less than the equivalent of two cents, and if the person approached by the beggar has no money — perhaps because he is a beggar himself — he has to refuse the panhandler in a civilized way.

More serious, however, before the 1971 split were the mass demonstrations and political unrest. The students of the University of Dacca, especially, worried about the future. Even after they received their diplomas, what could they do? They said that most of the good government jobs had been given to west-wing people.

Over and over again, the people of what was then the east wing voiced their grievances. They charged that the real power was in the hands of the rich men of West Pakistan, especially the owners of large estates. These "westerners," said the east people, were unfamiliar with the easterners' problems and looked down upon them. West Pakistan, according to the east, treated the smaller wing as a colony, not as an equal part of the same country. This treatment, as we know, eventually led to disaster.

(19)

DIFFERING CUSTOMS

The Bengalis are intensely proud of their land. A government publication states: "They [the Bengalis] are born artists and poets . . . deeply devoted to their families . . . relaxed, friendly, and social people, lightly built, swarthy, and full of the natural grace of those who live in close communion with nature."

Many men in Bangladesh wear the *lungi*, which resembles a skirt. It is made of colored cloth wound around the waist and extending to the ankles. It is worn with a collarless white tunic shirt. Many of the Hindus wear the *dhoti*, a long piece of white cotton, folded somewhat like trousers and tucked in at the waist. The traditional headgear in Bangladesh and Pakistan is the turban, a cap with a cotton or linen scarf wound around it. Some people — those who can afford it — in urban areas wear the Jinnah cap, a peaked headgear of lambskin or sheepskin, sometimes dressed with fur.

URBAN AREAS

Bangladesh is a land of small villages. Only a small part of the population lives in urban areas, but the country also has some important cities, in addition to Dacca.

Chittagong is to Bangladesh what Karachi is to Pakistan, its natural harbor and "lookout" on the world. It is located on the Karnafuli River, about a dozen miles from the Bay of Bengal. The population numbers more than half a million.

A sixteenth-century merchant-sailor called Chittagong "the most famous and wealthy city of the Kingdom of Bengal." It is famous today, too, and some of its citizens have great wealth, judging by their homes. But the city also has great poverty, as shown by the number of people who live in the streets.

The harbor of Chittagong is a mixture of old and new. Since Bangladesh moves largely in boats, local vessels in various shapes are common sights, especially the picturesque *ghashis* with their high masts and mat-roofed cabins. The harbor is always filled with freighters, too, from all over the world.

Right: the growing
residential district of Dacca.
Left: street scene in Dacca.

Among the most interesting sights in Chittagong is a slab in an old mosque, called Qadam Mubaric. The slab has an imprint that looks like a footprint, said to be that of the Prophet Muhammad, founder of the Islam religion. No one knows how the slab reached the city.

On the outskirts of Chittagong is another tourist attraction, a shrine filled with tortoises. Some people say that the creatures are sacred. Others claim that they originally had been *djinns* — evil spirits — but were changed into tortoises by a visiting holy man.

About twenty-five years ago, the city of Khulna was a small town with a population of about 30,000. Today its people number nearly half a million. Situated in the south, on one of the many arms of the Ganges River, it is a fast-developing industrial city. Eventually Khulna may absorb some of the surplus populations of Dacca and Chittagong.

The port of Chalna is some eighteen miles south of Khulna. It is the second harbor of Bangladesh.

THE WATER SUPPLY AND THE CLIMATE

While rain is scarce in much of Pakistan, it seems to fall in bucketfuls in Bangladesh. In certain northern areas, the rainfall reaches 200 inches a year, five times the amount on the eastern coast of the United States.

Rain is only one source of Bangladesh's immense water supply. Some of the most water-rich streams in the subcontinent provide the other sources. The largest of the streams are the Ganges and the Brahmaputra. Both originate in Tibet, some two miles above sea level, in what is sometimes called the Abode of Gods. Turning east, the Ganges (which becomes the Padma) first tries to encircle, then smashes through, the mountain ramparts, moving toward the sea. The Brahmaputra (which becomes the Jamuna), on the other hand, first runs westward, speeds and hurtles down the cliffs, and then moves southward.

Coming down from the north is still another river, the Meghna. It picks up the waters of the two giants, carrying them down into the Bay of Bengal, and forming a large and complex delta. It is particularly complex because the constant silting of the enormous amount of water brought down from the mountains changes the contours of the streams. At one point the banks of the Meghna were once 20 miles apart, a distance now reduced to 5 miles. Before entering the sea, the delta is some 280 miles wide, enclosing a third of East Bengal. When in flood, carrying the spring freshets of the glaciers, the combined rivers discharge nearly 1,800,000 cubic feet each second, which is more than the maximum of the Mississippi.

Terrible windstorms sometimes hit the Bengal coast. The Chinese call them *typhoons*, or "great winds." High-crested waves, known as *bores*, reverse the flow of the rivers, flooding the land. The ramshackle huts of the people collapse and animals are drowned. Often hundreds, and even thousands, of people die in this raging weather. The tidal waves of 1876 killed about 100,000 persons.

Perhaps the greatest natural disaster of this century hit Bangladesh on November 12–13, 1970. It came in the wake of 30-foot tidal waves, as the result of a cyclone, driven from the Bay of Bengal to pound 3,000 square miles of the delta. The official death toll was 200,000, with another 100,000 missing. But it is believed that 500,000 people may have died.

THE SUNDARBANS

Silt-charged delta waters have built up a 6,000-square-mile southern swamp region in Bangladesh. It is called *Sundarbans*, named after the tree of the region, the *sundri*. This is one of the few remaining natural sanctuaries for big game.

If Africa is today's land of the big game, the subcontinent was that in the past. In the Sundarbans, hunters still occasionally encounter the magnificent Bengal tiger, as well as leopards, wild boars, and other big game.

To protect their plots of land from too much water, the growers in this area have constructed networks of artificial embankments, called *bund*. They not only restrain the river but serve as a thoroughfare along the stream.

Remains of a
textile mill, destroyed
by a typhoon

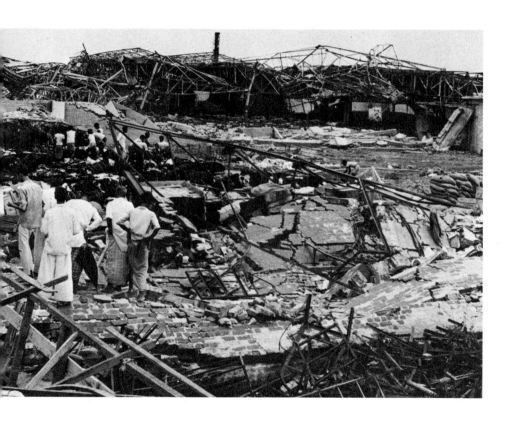

Terraced fields,
painstakingly carved
along the hilly slopes

THE THIRSTY PLANTS

In a region blessed with an overabundance of water, the "thirsty plants" have a chance to grow. These specialties of East Bengal need much water. The region is the largest producer and exporter of jute, which the United States, for one, buys in large quantities. *Jute* is a Bengal word meaning "matted hair," and so called because of the appearance of the glossy fiber. It is used to make many products, including twine, rope, burlap, sacking, and wrapping paper. Mixed with wool or silk, it can be used as a clothing fabric.

In the country's tropical and subtropical climate, rice, the staple of the land, prospers. Rice is believed to have originated in this area, developing into man's most important food. It is the main diet of about half of the people of the world, especially in the countries of Asia.

Another thirsty plant is tea, which Bangladesh produces in the north and parts of the south. In the north the tea gardens are on the slopes of the Sylhet hills, where some 200 inches of annual rainfall keep the soil humid and porous. Another important tea-producing region is in the southeast, near Chittagong.

The abundance of water in Bangladesh, and the lack of it in Pakistan, explain why Bengal, with less than one fifth of the land area of Pakistan, contains a larger population. It has more food to feed more people.

CHAPTER FIVE
THE RICH HISTORY OF THE SUBCONTINENT

The subcontinent already had a history of more than three thousand years, before the creed of the Prophet Muhammad reached the land. "Mound of the Dead" — Moenjodaro (Mohenjo Daro) — is the name of the excavated territory some two hundred miles north of the Arabian Sea, along the Indus. Covered by the desert sand, it had lain buried for thousands of years, to be excavated in 1922. It may be forty-five hundred years old, or even older.

The excavations have revealed a city in which the well-to-do resided in brick buildings, with baths and other conveniences. The city also had a drainage and sewer system. That is more than can be said of towns in the region today. Four hundred miles to the north of the Mound of the Dead, excavators found the remnants of another large city, called Harappa. Sixty settlements were strung out between the two urban areas.

Well-organized governing authorities protected these settlements. Their populations honored nature gods in impressive shrines. The rulers themselves lived in well-shielded palaces.

The people of the Harappa civilization had a written language, which has not yet been deciphered. Engraved seals, found at the sites, indicate that the area had heavier rainfall than it does today and that its vegetation was rich. The seals reproduce images of barley, wheat, field peas, cotton, and dates. They also show representations of tigers, elephants, and rhinos. The inhabitants held public markets and kept their food supplies in glazed pottery.

The Indus River, therefore, has been the center of an ancient civilization, along with the Nile in Egypt and the Tigris and Euphrates in today's Iraq. These rivers provided water and transportation. The flanking arid areas shielded the people against predatory bands.

However, the Harappa civilization died. Nobody knows when or how. The cities of the living became the Mounds of the Dead. This old civilization occupied the site of what is now Pakistan — a new country in an ancient land.

The subcontinent is protected by the tallest mountains in the world. But these ranges were no real obstacles to conquering hordes bent on grabbing this "magic land."

From the north of the mountains — in today's USSR — came the conquerors who finally took over the subcontinent. They crossed the ranges up to 1200 B.C., speaking an Aryan tongue.

The Harappa civilization may have been their victim. They pushed the natives southward, slaughtering many. The invaders brought their nature gods with them. They composed the devotional poems, known as the *Vedas,* and the philosophical thoughts in prose and verse, known as the *Upanishads.* These writings contain the basic points of the Hindu creed.

Many great conquerors were attracted to India. Consumed by burning ambition, driven by military genius, Alexander the Great (356–323 B.C.) conquered most of the known world while he was still in his twenties. He had become the master of Egypt and of Mesopotamia (Iraq). Then he burst into the valley of the Indus, in 327–325 B.C. He would have continued his conquering march, but his soldiers rebelled. Having reached the end of the world, as they saw it, and having been away from their European homes for years, they forced their leaders to turn around.

Alexander did not survive the retreat. He died in Baghdad, on the Tigris River, at the age of thirty-three. His life was short, but his fame was undying. In Pakistan, too, he is a legendary figure. Fathers still name their sons after him. "May the child be as valiant as his name-sake," they say.

The majority of the people on the subcontinent had become Hindus. In A.D. 711, Arab conquerors reached the land. They laid the foundations of today's Pakistan and Bangladesh.

The Arabs were led by a youth of seventeen — Muhammad-al-Qazim. He and his warriors landed on the coast at Daibul, near Karachi. These people were Muslims, whose Prophet Muhammad had proclaimed a century before that there was no god but Allah.

The Muslims had been desert-dwellers in the Arabian oasis town of Mecca. With the name of Allah on their lips, they had broken out of their isolation and spread the creed throughout the world. They were amazingly successful. In the very year when the Arabs landed in the Sind region, other Muslims crossed the Strait of Gibraltar and entered what is now Spain. They laid the foundations of the world's largest empire.

Under the leadership of the young warrior, the Muslims moved deep inland on the subcontinent. Many Hindus became Muslim converts. Those who remained Hindus paid a tax to the victors. The children of the newcomers and their converts became the ancestors of today's Pakistanis and Bengalis.

The first Muslim conquest was followed by many others. Spread over a wide arc of Central Asia, Turkic people had also become Muslims, and they now began to invade India.

The leader of the next large group of invaders was Mahmud of Ghazni (c. 971–1030). He invaded India beginning in 1001. As a Muslim, he detested the representations of Hindu gods and had them destroyed. And so he became known as the Idol Smasher. His fanatic opposition to Hinduism unleashed a feud between the followers of the two religions. Eventually this led to much communal strife. Mahmud extended his rule into the Punjab and established his capital at Lahore.

The Ghaznavidi, ruler heirs of Mahmud, were followed by other Muslims of Turkic origin. They had moved in from the Afghan lands. India's most fertile land is the broad valley of the Ganges, and the Muslim invaders penetrated into this area, capturing the city of Delhi.

The peninsula's attraction continued. The forces of Tamerlane (c. 1336–1405) — Timur the Lame — a descendant of Genghis Khan, invaded India in 1398, killing some 80,000 inhabitants of Delhi. It made no difference to him, a Muslim, that many Muslims were among his victims, too.

Dynasties followed one upon the other. The leaders were Muslims, but the majority of their subjects were Hindus. The time was right for a strong man to gain the throne.

In the sixteenth century, the man appeared. He was Zahir ud-Din Muhammad (1483–1530), a descendant of Tamerlane. He is best known as Babur the Tiger.

Babur was fourteen when he waged war on the rulers of Samarkand, a central Asian oasis city and an important caravan hub on the route from China to the West. He had been twelve when he ascended to the throne of Fergana, another central Asian city-state (in today's USSR). Because of his Mongolian heritage, the ruling family is known as the Mogul Dynasty.

At eighteen, Babur was a veteran of many wars. India now attracted him, as it had attracted other great warriors. "He who sits down to the feast of life," he said, "must end by drinking the cup of death."

In 1526 Babur defeated the much larger army of Ibrahim Lodi, an Afghan sultan, near Panipat, some miles from Delhi. He established the Mogul Dynasty, which lasted until modern times.

Babur extended his reign over northern and central India and beyond, into the Afghans' land. The name of the Moguls has entered the dictionaries of many languages. Today, the word means "a great personage."

A cruel man, Babur lived up to his reputation. Once an attempt was made to put poison into his food, but the plot was discovered in time. In his raging fury, the "Tiger" had his cook flayed alive, his official "taster" cut to pieces, and two female kitchen aides trampled to death by elephants.

Yet this cruel ruler could be fair and kind, too. Most of his sub-

Tomb of Shah Rukn-e-Alam,
Timur's fourth son,
at Multan, Pakistan

jects were Hindus, whom he treated well, launching large public-works projects. He was also a sensitive man in some respects. He liked to listen to poets. Poetic contests, called *mushaira,* are still popular in Pakistan today. He wrote sensitive poetry both in Persian and Turkic, and he was called *bülbül* — "nightingale" — by courtiers.

For the enjoyment of his subjects, Babur opened public gardens. A lover of nature, he was said to know the name of every flower in his vast realm. His favorite flowers were tulips, of which he himself cultivated more than thirty varieties. Because of his background, they seem to have been particularly close to him. Tulips are believed to have originated in Turkic lands. Their name is of Turkish origin, from *turban,* an Oriental headgear that these flowers resemble.

Babur lived only four years after his great victory at Panipat. But during that short time he laid the foundations of a vast empire. Yet it was his grandson who gave India its golden age.

His real name was Jalul-ud-Din Muhammad (1556–1605), but history knows him as Akbar the Great. He attempted to solve the subcontinent's great problem — the relations of the Muslim and Hindu communities. His rule lasted for half a century.

Akbar was a boy of fourteen when he ascended a shaky Mogul throne. Four years later, he was in full control. Because of his remarkable military achievements, he has been compared with Julius Caesar and Napoleon the Great.

Akbar knew that one of his main tasks was to make the Hindus and Muslims live in peace. He was himself a Muslim, had married a Hindu princess, and encouraged Christians to come into his country to teach in the schools. He also encouraged followers of other religions — Buddhists, Parsees, Sikhs — to make their contributions. Indeed, he attempted to combine all these faiths, establishing a common creed for the people, which he called Din-i-Ilabi — the Faith of God.

Akbar discouraged some of the practices that struck him as the scourges of India. Parents were in the habit of betrothing and even marrying off their children before they were ten years old. Akbar frowned on this practice. Hindu wives whose husbands died were expected to climb the funeral pyres of their late spouses and be burned alive. Akbar sought to have the people abandon their funeral rite.

Akbar's son, Sultan Selim, adopted the name of Jahangir (1569–1627) — Conqueror of the World. But he was not even the ruler in his own palace. The real ruler was his wife, a Persian woman whom he called the Light of the Palace and Light of the World.

Jahangir's heir was Shah Jahan (1592–1666) — King of the World — and he was not much better than his father. However, the world remembers him, not for any statesmanlike deeds, but because he built the Taj Mahal, the mausoleum for his favorite wife, Mumtaz Mahal, at the city of Agra. It is exquisitely proportioned and decorated in the Muslim-Arab style, its stunning white dome flanked by four lacy minarets. The Taj Mahal seems to float on air.

The Mogul Empire reached its largest extension under Jahan's son, Aurangzeb (1618–1707). But his reign was also the beginning of the end for the dynasty. Aurangzeb did not know how to deal with Hindus. A fanatic Muslim, he had the Hindu shrines destroyed. As before, Hindus had to bear the burden of crushing taxes. More than ever, the Muslim upper class — self-confident and martial — ruled over a disorganized majority of Hindus. Aurangzeb ruled until 1707, when his reign ended in anarchy.

BRITAIN IN INDIA

India had attracted conquerors not only from central Asia but also from western Europe — the Portuguese, the French, and the British. The subcontinent was the supplier of luxury products that the wealthy of Europe wanted: spices, silk, and gems.

As the Mogul Dynasty weakened, the British moved in. They formed the East India Company, or Governor and Company of Merchants Trading into the East Indies. The company operated under a charter granted by the British government.

The main function of the company was trading. But this activity was hampered by the constant feuding among the local rulers, whose

Left: tomb of Jahingir's wife.
Right: the Aurangabad Palace
in India, commonly known
as Lalbagh Fort, was built by
Prince Muhammad Azam Khan,
third son of Aurangzeb.

power grew as the Moguls weakened. The feuds degenerated into anarchy. For the sake of its business, the British company wanted law in the land. Several princes also welcomed British attempts to introduce order for their own protection against their neighbors. Thus Britain extended its rule.

India had a population of countless millions. Through the I.C.S. — Indian Civil Service — the British ruled with a small but effective bureaucracy of a few thousand. Since they were in a tiny minority, they employed the age-old device of "divide and rule," playing on the jealousies of the native princes and the religious communities. The Muslims had been the rulers over the best parts of India, particularly in the fertile Gangetic Plains. Therefore the British sought to weaken the Muslims. The Hindus had been the weaker, even though they were in a great majority. Therefore the British sought to strengthen them. Many doors that were closed to the Muslims were opened to the Hindus — schools, jobs, land, and businesses.

At first the Indian Civil Service consisted of people who probably were not competent enough to succeed in their fields at home. Later the British improved the quality of the service. Officials were given stiff examinations. In the main, these people were confident and efficient. But most of them treated the subcontinent's population as inferior people. The Muslims were considered even more inferior than the Hindus, in line with the official policy of divide and rule.

Yet the British introduced many improvements into the country. They built a network of canals in what became the Islamic Republic, one of their most ambitious projects, as well as roads and rails, and they fostered farm production and trade.

Eventually India became the pivot of the British Empire. The government in London looked at world problems from a new angle: how would they affect Britain's position in the subcontinent?

In 1857 word spread among the Indian soldiers in Bengal that the cartridges of the new muzzle-loading Enfield weapons were greased with the fat of cows and pigs. The soldiers had to bite off the ends of the cartridges to pour the released powder into the barrels. Touching the fat of the cow was a defilement for the Hindu soldier, and tasting the fat of the pig was abomination for the Muslims. Their religions forbade them to touch these fats.

Shortly before this, the British had lost a campaign against the Afghans, India's neighbors, and thus had lost face. About the same time, Britain had annexed several Indian princely states. They also forbade the killing of unwanted baby girls, and the traditional suicide of Hindu widows on their husbands' funeral pyres. All of these British steps irked many people, still attached to ancient ways.

Then, suddenly, a riot by Indian soldiers flared up in Bengal in 1857. It spread into the Ganges Valley, especially in Delhi. The British responded, and a vicious war broke out called the Sepoy Mutiny.

The brunt of the fight on the British side was on a small contingent of troops. The Indian soldiers were in a majority. Most of the civilian people of India — the peasants — remained aloof. But some Indian princes helped the British. They feared that Britain's defeat would lead to anarchy.

In the end, the British won and the Moguls lost their shadow throne. Power was now transferred from the East India Company to the British crown. The secretary of state for India in the London government became the top official of the subcontinent.

After the mutiny, India consisted of two unequal parts — British India, which had a majority of the population, and the India of the princes, of whom there were close to six hundred. In the former the British ruled directly through the I.C.S. In the latter the princes had self-government in internal matters, with the "advice" of the British. Often the "advice" was more important than the princes' decisions. In foreign policy, defense, and finances, the British had the final words in the princely states, too. In the course of time, the Indian Civil Service became an elite body, manned by some truly excellent officials. But no matter how excellent they were, educated Indians came to see the system as unjust, because the Indians, forming the vast majority, were still treated as inferiors.

Many Indians had been educated in England, and the autocratic rule in their native land was of great concern to them. In order to have a voice in the administration of their country, they set up an organization of their own, in 1885, with the help of a sympathetic Englishman, Allan Octavian Hume. They called it the Indian National Congress. It was to include Indians of all creeds, Hindus, Muslims, and others, and they were to work for a more democratic system in India.

The wars and the revolutions that broke out in the twentieth century indirectly helped the Indians. World War I was fought, in the words of the President of the United States, Woodrow Wilson, to "make the world safe for democracy." India was a part of that world; indeed, a very large part. The articulate people of India took the words of Wilson seriously and called for the rule of democracy.

Before the war was over, Russia had gone Communist. One of its propaganda devices was to call on the peoples of the colonies to "strike off their fetters." This anticolonial doctrine had a strong echo in India. Subsequently, the British had to admit some Indian representatives into the government councils of the subcontinent. But the government was still far from democratic.

After World War I, the name of Mohandas Karamchand Gandhi began to be heard. He was a frail-looking Indian lawyer with a weak, reedy voice. Yet he impressed the world as a giant and his voice was noted around the globe. India must be free, Gandhi said, but not by violence. That, he declared, solved no problems and only begot new ones. He proclaimed the rule of *ahimsa,* nonviolence, and the irrepressible force of truth, *satyagraha.*

Gandhi spoke for both the Hindus and the Muslims within the Congress party and played a major role in it. At the same time, the Muslims also set up their own organization, called the League.

World War II broke out, and again the British were involved. To ensure the loyalty of the Indians, Britain offered them independence after the war.

Meanwhile, a poet had put an idea into the Muslims' heads and it had a historic sequel. The poet was Muhammad Iqbal. He wrote his verses in English, Persian, and Urdu, the popular tongue in the Punjab-

Kashmir frontierland where he was born in 1873. He was a man of both East and West, having obtained his doctorate in philosophy at the University of Munich in Germany.

In a speech in 1930, Iqbal said that Islam and Hinduism were two completely different ways of life, and, therefore, independent India should be divided into two nations.

This idea appealed to many Muslims. One of them, Choudry Rahmat Ali, a disciple of Iqbal's, suggested the name for the Muslim portion of the subcontinent. It should be called Pakistan — "land of the pure." Also, the name contained the first letters of what would be the parts of the country: P(unjab); A(fghan; North-West Territory); K(ashmir); I(slam); S(ind); and the Persian word for country — *tan*.

MOHAMMED ALI JINNAH

Great Britain was at the peak of its power when Mohammed Ali Jinnah was born in 1876. That was the year when Britain's Queen Victoria assumed the title of *Kaiser-i-Hind*, empress of India.

"Jinnah" means the "lean one," and that he remained all his life. He came from a Muslim family, but did not practice his religion. In line with the custom then prevailing, he was betrothed before fifteen. His wife died at a young age.

Jinnah's father, a rich merchant, could afford to send him to Britain, where the careers of many young Indians were made. He was sixteen at the time. He studied law and did very well in school. Although a native-born Indian, the only language he spoke fluently was English, and he learned the ways of an English gentleman.

Returning home, Jinnah started to practice law and became highly successful. He married out of his Muslim community. His second wife was a Parsee, a member of a small sect.

Jinnah was an ambitious and willful man, who wanted to make a successful career in politics, too. If India was to have self-government, he wanted a share of power. He joined the Indian National Congress, but found the organization dominated by Hindus.

Right: Gandhi preached nonviolence.
Left: Mohammed Ali Jinnah.

Gandhi held that the union of the two great religious communities was essential for the subcontinent. Jinnah thought that India under Gandhi's influence was bound to be dominated by the Hindus.

As independence approached, Jinnah broke with the Congress party and advocated the partition of the subcontinent into Pakistan and India. The former would contain the majority of the Muslims. He knew, of course, that the parts were not contiguously settled. The bulk of the Muslim population lived at the extreme ends of the peninsula. Gandhi said that the division was absurd. Jinnah said it was inevitable. Gandhi tried hard to convince Jinnah that both Muslims and Hindus would benefit by a united India. Religions were important, he said, but they no longer were the foundations of countries. A modern country must have a system in which "church" and state are separate.

But Jinnah insisted that India was different because, in fact, the religion of its majority did form the foundation of life. Besides, in a united India the Hindus would exert the dominant influence. They were better educated, and skilled in business and government duties. Over and over again he repeated that only as the citizens of two separate nations could the Muslims and Hindus work together.

Jinnah took his beliefs to the people. The differences between him and his countrymen were enormous. He stood before the crowds like an English gentleman, in an elegantly tailored suit and wearing a monocle. Most of his audience did not even understand his Cambridge English.

Whatever fire may have been in Jinnah, it was not revealed in his public appearances. He had a cool, dispassionate personality. Sometimes he would speak for hours, while his audience — understanding little of what he said — seemed to be enthralled. To them he was a prophet, a man of destiny. Farmers, herders, craftsmen, and domestic servants listened to him and wanted change. Their most precious possession was Islam. They called for their own Muslim nation.

The Muslim people of India would have followed Jinnah wherever he led them. They trusted him. He was their spokesman, the promise of a great and glorious future. They accepted his idea of a separate nation — the Islamic Republic with two wings.

THE PARTITION

World War II was over. The Allies had won, but Britain was now losing an empire. The British finally agreed to their colonies' demands for freedom.

Since the Muslims and Hindus could not agree on a united country, two nations were created. Lord Mountbatten, statesman, soldier, and member of British royalty, carried out the transfer of power. It took place at midnight, August 14, 1947. Two nations were born, India and the Islamic State of Pakistan, which in a few years changed to the Islamic Republic of Pakistan. The seaport city of Karachi became the capital of the new Muslim country, and New Delhi was named the capital of India.

The Republic's new flag was dark green, with a white vertical stripe at the hoist, and a white crescent and five-pointed star in the center. Green was the color of the Prophet and the crescent is the emblem of Islam. The flag, as well as the new anthem, stressed the fact that the nation was dedicated to Islam and its founder. (Pakistan retained its flag after the 1971 split; the flag of Bangladesh is solid green with a red circle in the center.)

But even before the two countries were established, terrible events took place. Driven by the fear of falling under foreign rule, suddenly millions of people began to move, migrating into the Islamic Republic from India and the other way around. Squeezed in between the two communities were the Sikhs, who lived mainly in the Punjab. Never had history seen so vast a migration in so short a time. How many people were on the move nobody knows — 12 million or perhaps more. They became refugees in crowded slums of indescribable squalor.

Then, in a frightful outburst of hatred, the migrants began to slaughter one another — Hindus, Muslims, and Sikhs. The violent outbreak was caused by many things: fear, hunger, the summer heat. "A thousand shall fall," says the Bible, but nobody was able to count the dead in this holocaust. The number is estimated from 100,000 to more than a million. After months of fighting the bloodshed finally ended from sheer exhaustion.

THE PERIOD OF UNITY

The Islamic Republic of Pakistan was established as an independent sovereign state with dominion status. This meant that it was an equal partner with Britain and others in the Commonwealth of Nations, formerly the British Empire.

Jinnah became the first governor-general (president) of the country. At that time he was already a sickly man. A year after the birth of his nation, he died of a lung ailment.

The economic disadvantages of partition were soon proven. The Islamic Republic had most of the raw jute, but India had the factories. The new nation had cotton, wheat, and rice, but India had most of the cotton-ginning, pressing, spinning, and weaving mills, as well as flour mills, sugar refineries, tobacco factories, and rice mills. The Islamic Republic produced hides and skins, but India had the leatherworks. India had the most skilled people, since more Hindus than Muslims had been trained in finance and administration and government services. Far more of them were college-educated, too. Many Muslims had been trained for the armed services, and they lost their jobs when India went its own way.

On the other hand, large numbers of Muslims were *zamindars* — landlords — who wanted nothing to change. Change might have meant land reform and the loss of their estates.

In the wake of partition, other troubles arose. How were the two nations to divide the assets and liabilities inherited from the British? How many locomotives and planes should go to the Republic? How many writing desks and inkstands should go to India? It took years to untie the knots.

After Jinnah's death, there was no one to hold his Muslim League together. And so it began to fall apart. The opposition — particularly the Awami party, advocating reforms on the Soviet model — was gaining ascendancy. In the east, the Bengalis insisted that the west paid little attention to them and that it "robbed" the east. Liaquat Ali Khan, a longtime associate of Jinnah's and an able lawyer, stepped forward as the head of government. But he lacked his predecessor's skill and personality. In 1951 he was assassinated by a political fanatic.

Unlike India, where state and religion were separated, the Islamic Republic had become an Islamic state. Its substitute for a constitution — the Basic Principles Report — prescribed that only a Muslim could become the head of state. The law of the land was based upon the sacred scripts of the creed — the Koran — composed in the seventh century. The law prohibited drinking, gambling, the charging of interest, and many other things. How was a country to run in which capital was not available? Before a bill could become a law, a board of Muslim scholars had to give its approval.

Meanwhile, provincial elections were held. Some of the opposition members were jailed and the police were said to have harassed others. Paid informers and secret police were everywhere. Taxes were heavy on the poor and light on the rich. Charges were made that officials could be bought, government contracts obtained through bribery, and export and import licenses traded to the highest bidders. In 1953 the authorities revealed that in the canal-irrigated granary of the Punjab, people had to eat grass to live. The dream of independence became a nightmare.

It was impossible to make advances in any direction without first breaking the rich landowners' monopoly of power. One tenth of them owned 15 percent of the land in the western section. The holdings of most of the farmers were so tiny that they could not make a living.

Suddenly, in the fall of 1958, the commander of the armed forces, General Mohammed Ayub Khan, seized power to reorganize the regime. Ayub Khan, Pakistan's strong man, looked, spoke, and acted like a no-nonsense British army officer, which he was by training and education. Born in northwest India, he received his military education at Sandhurst, Britain's outstanding military academy. During World War II he was one of two Muslim officers in command of British units.

Now Ayub Khan wanted to end the corrupt practices, which he said ravaged the country. He wanted to have more people own land. Also, he wanted to train more people for intelligent decision-making in politics. He felt that the "democracy" of the previous regime was autocracy in disguise. It was better, he said, to have an honest political system in strong hands than a false democracy.

Left: citizens marking
ballots in Dacca.
Right: Ayub Khan
greeting the people.

Right: plowing a wheat field.
Left: these housewives
are going back to school.

"Let me announce," he said, ". . . that our ultimate aim is to restore democracy, but of the type people can understand and work. Millions of ignorant people do not add up to a well-informed nation."

Ayub Khan established a system called Basic Democracies, under which several tiers of popularly elected councils were set up. The first was the Union Council, with one elected representative for every one thousand to fifteen hundred people, the size of an average village. People in the next-highest tier elected representatives of the subdistricts, and the next ones of the districts and divisions. The country's two wings each received an advisory council. Some 80,000 "basic democrats" were to choose the president at the next national election.

Under Ayub Khan, the Islamic Republic introduced several economic plans, mainly for five-year periods. The resources of the government and private individuals were to be used for the greater benefit of the greatest number of people. Precedence was given to agriculture, the basic occupation of the country. The river system of the west was used for irrigation, and the dams for power. Factories were set up for processing raw materials — jute, sugar, cotton, and chemicals. Other plants were to produce fertilizers, drugs, paper, steel, and ships. The country was explored for mineral deposits. More roads were built and schools opened.

In the previous government, 55 to 70 percent of the national budget had been spent on the armed forces and only 1 percent on education. Expenditures for primary education were increased 60 percent under Ayub Khan's rule. He called his method the Total Approach Plan because no major national problem was overlooked.

A system of land reform was introduced, too. The owners of large holdings were allowed to retain only 1,000 acres of nonirrigated and 500 acres of irrigated land. Farmers were encouraged to buy land, with government help.

Unfortunately, however, not even Ayub Khan could make much headway against the resistance of the *zamindars*. They "divided" their land, on paper, among their relatives, thus escaping the law's restrictions. Only a little over 2 million acres became available under the land reform law, distributed among 150,000 tenants.

In 1968, the tenth anniversary of Ayub Khan's rule, he became the target of his people's attacks. Their living conditions improved too slowly, they charged. Student disorders broke out. East Pakistan voiced its old accusation that it was treated as a mere colony. The demonstrators shouted that corruption was once again rampant in the country. An attempt was made on Ayub's life, but he escaped unharmed.

Ten years before, Ayub Khan had been helped into power by his close associate, General Agha Mohammed Yahya Khan. Now this general toppled his old friend. Yahya Khan became the new president.

The son of an aristocratic family from the northwest, Yahya Khan was a graduate of the Indian Military Academy and founder of the Pakistan Staff College.

His first pronouncements were that the eastern section would get more government funds and that corruption would be rooted out. He promised nationwide elections for a constituent assembly to frame a new constitution. He also promised to retire as head of the nation once his mission was accomplished, turning over the government to civilians.

In 1970, the country began its fourth five-year plan. The government pledged to double its contribution to what is now Bangladesh, which was to receive three fourths of the increased funds, in order to speed up progress.

Plans to improve the condition of the people went ahead. The huge Manghla Dam on the Jhelum River was hailed as the largest earth-fill dam in the world, with an artificial lake forty miles long, and a capacity to irrigate 3 million acres, as well as to provide cheap power.

On independence day in 1947, the people of the Islamic Republic had an average life expectancy of thirty-five years. By the mid-1970s it was around fifty years in Pakistan and Bangladesh, improved, but still very low when compared with the United States figure of seventy years. Also in 1947, the new nation's people were among the poorest in the world, with an average yearly income of $40 per person. Twenty-five years later the average income in the two countries was said to be $120 per person.

CHAPTER SIX
RELIGION IN THE TWO COUNTRIES

As if on command, tens of thousands of people rise from the ground and prostrate themselves again. The place is the large courtyard of Lahore's Great Mosque. *Mosque* means "bowing down." The worshipers are Muslims, followers of Islam, which means submission to the will of Allah. Most Pakistans and Bengalis are Muslims.

Inside the mosque the only decorations are the delicately patterned carpets, on which the devout perform their religious exercises. There is a niche in the wall, called *mihrab,* showing the direction to Mecca, in Arabia, the city in which the creed was born.

At the beginning of the seventh century, Muhammad told his fellow townsmen in Mecca that they were wrong to venerate their nature gods. There was only one god, he said, and He was Allah. Muhammad told them that Allah had ninety-nine attributes, indicating that He was the ruler in all the heavens. In Allah's eyes, all people were equal.

The creeds of the idol-worshipers were complex. They did not know whom to flatter among the many gods, and to which of them to offer sacrifices. Nor did they know which priesthood of the gods to appease. In contrast, Islam was a simple creed, with no priesthood. The Muslim had only to proclaim that there was but one god, and Muhammad was His prophet; to pray five times a day; to distribute alms to the poor; to observe the month-long festival of Ramazan (Ramadan), and to make a pilgrimage to Mecca, cradle of the faith, if he could afford it. Islam is not a complex religion.

The simple approach of the new religion appealed to an increasing number of people. There were many converts. Islam is still growing today, replacing idol worship, for instance, in large parts of Africa.

Millions of Hindus still remain in Pakistan and Bangladesh. As against the one god of the Muslims, the Hindus, their neighbors, have innumerable deities. Most of them are local gods — of villages, castes, and clans — and not all are endowed with human features. Three stand out, members of the *trimurti* (triad, or trinity): Brahma, creator of the world, after whom Brahmanism (another word for Hinduism) is named; Vishnu the Preserver; and Siva the Destroyer.

In contrast to the Muslims' belief in the equality of all men before Allah, the Hindus believe in a caste system. There are four major castes: priestly, knightly, merchant, and menial. They, in turn, are divided into countless subcastes. Members of the different castes are not supposed to intermarry or even dine together. Contact with lower castes means defilement, which calls for purification rites. Below the castes are those who do not belong to any castes and were therefore called in the past outcastes, or pariahs. India's great leader Gandhi called them *harijans,* children of God.

While the Muslim believes in only one life, followed by hell or paradise, the Hindu believes in countless rounds of lives, due to the *samsara,* transmigration of the soul. One may be a prince in this existence and then, possibly, a snake in the next, as punishment for past misdeeds. Or it may be the other way around.

The Hindu venerates the cow; the Muslim eats its meat. To the Hindu some rivers are sacred; not to the Muslim. And there are many other differences in worship and everyday life.

In rural societies, especially in developing countries, people eagerly look forward to holidays as diversions in their hard lives. Holidays are social occasions for gaiety. These holidays, too, reveal the differences between the Muslim and the Hindu.

To the Muslim the ninth month of his lunar year is sanctified. In that month Muhammad received the Koran, the sacred script, from Allah, through the Archangel Gabriel. It is a month of fasting and

feasting — fasting during the hours of daylight and feasting by night. This is Ramazan.

It is followed by a particularly joyous holiday, *Id-al-Fitr*, lasting three days. People put on new clothes, exchange visits, and attend the graves of relatives. The *Id-al-Azha*, Festival of Sacrifice, commemorates the test of Abraham by Allah. Abraham was to sacrifice his son, but Allah did not want the death of the boy. Joyously, Abraham sacrificed a ram in his place. On that holiday people kill lambs, feast on the meat, and give the rest to the poor. During this holiday period, those who can afford it make their pilgrimages — called *hajj* — to Mecca and return with the title of *hajji*, having the right to wear a special turban.

Since the Hindus have so many gods, their holidays are numerous, too. Many celebrations are in honor of Lord Krishna, one of the favorites, and others honor goddesses of wealth and knowledge. A particularly popular holiday is the *holi*, a fertility rite in early spring, with street dancing, bonfires, and general gaiety. The *dasahara (dusserah)* celebrates the end of the monsoon, when masked street dancers act out the triumph of good over evil. Another popular festival is *dewali* — "row of lanterns" — in honor of the goddess Kali, whose victory over the demons is celebrated by a display of lights.

Although Islam is supposed to have no priests, there are people who perform priestly functions. The *ulema (mullah* in the singular), and priests under other names, may not be learned people. Some of them depend on the superstitions of their followers, selling them amulets, healing herbs, and charms.

Islam is not supposed to have any saints either. But there are many saints in the two countries, the so-called *pirs*. These people may be dead or alive. Both living and dead saints are supposed to perform miracles. Some of the living pirs have inherited their positions, while others have bought theirs. Pilgrimages — *urs* — to the tombs of famous pirs may be very profitable to the saints, their descendants, or managers, because of the contributions the pilgrims make. Often celebrated in a carnival spirit, with marketplace booths all over the premises, the pilgrimages to the tombs of the more famous saints attract thousands from all over the lands.

The number of pirs is particularly large in the province of Sind, in Pakistan. Happy is the village that can boast of a major saint — dead or alive. The pilgrimages to his tomb or to his sanctuary mean money and fame to the village people.

Some places, in the past, seem to have resorted to strong measures to obtain pirs of their own. A British government official, for instance, reported this event in a Sind village toward the end of the nineteenth century.

The village had no pir. Some of the villagers paid a visit to a man with a saintly reputation in a neighboring village to induce him, with all kinds of promises, to become the pir of their town. He accepted. When the holy man was settled, the townspeople wanted to be sure that he would never leave. With that in mind, they killed him and gave him a magnificent funeral. Then they made his tomb a place of pilgrimage, praying for his help in times of stress. The pir evidently responded, because his tomb brought in great profit to the local residents.

Originally, Islam shunned all complications. It insisted that there should be only one simple creed and the simplest of rites. Not only did it shun the priesthood, it shunned religious orders, too. But today there are religious orders in Pakistan and Bangladesh.

Members of the orders originally wore woolen garments, which gave them their name — *sufi,* meaning "wool." Within the orders are *murshids* — "masters" — who are instructors of the *murids* — "disciples." They are trying to find the path — *tariqat* — to virtuous life. Some countries call the order members *dervishes.* These people have various ways of seeking religious ecstasy, such as working themselves into a frenzy while whirling, dancing, or singing.

Where there is one god and only one prophet speaking for him, there is no need for separate sects. But there are such sects in these Muslim countries. The Shi'as are one. The word means "partisans," since they are ardent followers of Ali, the prophet's son-in-law. Mem-

bers of this sect worship Ali almost as if he were a god. Their great holiday is Moharram (Muharram), which means "sacred" in Arabic. It is the name of a month during which Ali's son, Husain, is said to have suffered martyrdom. On the tenth of the month, devotees carry a replica of the martyr's tomb — *tazia* — in a solemn procession. Often the participants in the procession slash away at themselves with swords, so as to share the pains of martyrdom.

Bangladesh extends into the part of Southeast Asia in which Buddhism predominates. There are about half a million Buddhists there. That religion grew out of Hinduism as a reform movement, some twenty-five centuries ago.

The founder of the creed was Siddhartha Gautama, a young prince in a small country on the southern Himalayan slopes. He believed that people should look for the divine spark in themselves, instead of in the shrines of Hindu gods. Looking into himself, he thought that he had found the solution to the great question of life. Why were people always suffering? They suffered because of their unworthy desires. These desires, he said, could be eliminated by way of the Eightfold Path — thought, meditation, motives, speech, effort, living action, resolve, and means of livelihood. He concluded that the ultimate goal of the virtuous man was *nirvana,* the absolute end of all passion and union with the supreme being in a condition of pure bliss.

In both India and Pakistan live the Sikhs, followers of still another religion. A learned man, Guri Nanak, founded the creed in the fifteenth century to reconcile the Muslims and Hindus in tolerant religious practices and to eliminate caste distinctions. It rejected the enormous number of Hindu gods. In the course of time, the Sikhs became a separate community. Eventually they forgot the basic thought of their founder — mutual tolerance.

CHAPTER SEVEN
VILLAGE LIFE

Punjabpur is one of the thousands of villages in the countries of Pakistan and Bangladesh. Although the villages are different in many respects, they are alike in one — each has a mosque. Five times a day the reedy-voiced *muezzin* — "caller" — proclaims that *Allaho-akbar* — "God is the greatest" — and invites the faithful to prayer.

This village is located in Pakistan, between the Chenab and Ravi rivers. Multan, the largest city in the area, is some sixty miles away. About half a dozen miles from Punjabpur is a sandy road, on which a couple of dusty buses maintain contact with the outside world. When the rains are scanty, Punjabpur is covered with a film of sand. The arid area is not far away.

When there is rain, however, mud is everywhere. Then it is particularly hard to distinguish the village from its environment. Clinging to an outcropping of rock, so as not to use up fertile farmland, the village seems to blend into the mud and rock.

Punjabpur is surrounded by a low wall of mud, which once may have served as protection. Now a small cannon could blast it away. But the wall seems to give the villagers a sense of security. This part of the subcontinent used to be the highway for invading armies from all parts of the world. People in a sleepy village such as this seem almost to live in another age.

Beautiful pottery
from Multan

The houses of Punjabpur are made of mud, too, except for the one belonging to the *agha*, the local rich man, who is also the *choudry*, or headman. His house is built of brick, faced with blue-streaked faïence, or glazed clay. Blue is believed to bring good luck.

The huts of the village are roofed with thatch, exuding a sweetish odor. Pats of buffalo dung, collected as fuel for chilly winter nights, cling to the outside walls.

Several huts are attached — glued together — to serve as homes for large families — parents, sons and their families, and unmarried daughters. The huts have no glass windows. They would be too costly. The window openings are small to keep out bad weather. The room is bare of furniture except for some cots called *charpoys*, some rugs, and essential household utensils and farm tools. The charpoy consists of wooden frames strung together with ropes, serving as a bedstead or chair. The floor of the hut is compacted mud, kept clean with buffalo dung. Hanging from the ceiling, out of the reach of the children and, it is hoped, insects, are a few clay jugs or stone-lined bins, the family granary, or food for lean days. The modest valuables of the family are hidden in a hollowed-out place in the wall, well concealed.

The 2,000 people of this village are nearly all Muslims. Most of their lives takes place in the courtyards and the fields. Protected by the walls of the huts, the women and children spend their days in the courtyards, except when the monsoon drives them indoors. Out in the open is the hearth, also made of mud, and the utensils needed for the preparation of the food. The women grind the grain while talking about local events. An ancient pipal tree may offer shade in the courtyard, and a banyan tree, with its numerous roots, may be nearby, too.

There are not many trees in the village. They have been cut down for fuel. There are no flowers. Even if the blossoms could stand the heat, they would not have enough water. Also, flowers are not for poor men, the villagers believe. They provide neither shade nor food.

Small children play in the courtyard. Their most popular game is *pir Kaudi*. It has a finish line, which a child tries to reach, while two others, whom he tries to tag, want to tackle him. If he reaches the line by sidestepping them, he wins. Then the game begins again.

The women go to the wells in groups when the men are away in the fields. Carrying jugs on their heads, and others in their hands, they move toward the well in single file. They walk gracefully and evenly, balancing the jugs. If there are trees nearby, the women take advantage of the shade they provide and sit down to await their turn at the well. While drawing water, they take their time, talking and often singing.

Back in their courtyards again, they prepare the food for the evening meal. Pakistan's most important staple is wheat, while that of Bangladesh is rice. The unleavened bread, *chappati,* is a favored food of Pakistan. The main dish for many people is *dal,* pealike lentils spiced with pepper and soaked in clarified butter, called *ghee.* Tea is a popular drink. Meat is rarely served in poorer homes, perhaps once a week, if at all, or on festive occasions, such as weddings and religious holidays.

Men and women live separately in Muslim lands, holding on to old ways. Poor people cannot live separately, since they have only one room for the entire family. Also, they have to work together in the fields.

For richer people, who can afford to live in homes with more than one room, there may be special quarters for women. There only their husbands and close male relatives can see them. The name of the women's quarters is *zenana,* from the Persian word for woman. Another name for the women's quarters in Muslim countries is *harem,* from the Arabic word *harim,* which means "forbidden, or secret."

Some women observe the *purdah,* which means "screen," because they are hidden from men's eyes. Women living this way wear a garment, a *burqah,* which completely covers them from head to toe (except for a slit for their eyes). In the streets these women look like "walking tents."

But modern people in the two countries live no differently than most Western women. They have no harem, do not observe the

Right: girls studying at
Eden Girls' College, Dacca.
Left: popular dress
among the wealthy urban
women of Pakistan.

purdah, and do not wear the burqah. They wear no veils either, as is still the custom in some Muslim lands where people hold on to the old ways.

At home, in the courtyard, women wear a pajamalike garment — *shalwargamiz* — including a bodice with long sleeves, reaching below the knees, and completed by the *dupatta*, a large scarf over the shoulders used to cover the head.

According to the Muslim sacred script, a man may have up to four wives if he can treat all of them equally well. Because of the high cost of living, few people can afford to support more than one wife. But even if a man wants to have a second wife, he must obtain the first wife's consent, and also that of the family court. Modern Pakistanis and Bengalis consider this practice of having many wives, known as polygamy, to be part of another, ancient world.

In Western countries during the 1970s, many women began to protest against such things as unequal pay and unequal opportunities. In these two lands, on the other hand, there was a built-in system of discrimination against women. As they were "screened," they became isolated. They could not even share the same school benches with boys. Far fewer girls go to school, anyway, than do boys. Women are not usually allowed to work together with men in most occupations in Pakistan or Bangladesh.

But change shows signs of reaching there, too. An increasing number of young women are trying to do away with the screen. A number of women are being admitted into such professions as medicine, law, and the arts. Fatimah Jinnah, sister of the Islamic Republic's founder, once even became candidate (an unsuccessful one, it turned out) for the office of president.

While the women of the village do their chores, the men are at work in the fields. In Pakistan they wear cotton trousers — *shalwar* — colored white or gray. They are full at the top, gathered at the waist, and tapered at the ankles. As well, they wear cotton shirts — *kurtas* — also white or gray, which are not tucked into the trousers. When the air is chilly, sleeveless sweaters are worn.

The fields surround the village, and the farmers have only short distances to go to work. Some have their own strips of land, mostly very small. Others work for the rich man of the village, getting a share of the crop, usually one fourth. They are sharecroppers and are among the poorest of people.

The farmers' tools are simple wooden plows. Peasants with their own buffalos are considered rich. With these primitive tools, the farmers' work is truly backbreaking. But there are welcome rest spells in the heat of the day.

In Muslim countries, men take prayer breaks. About the time that the village muezzin calls people to worship, the workers in the fields spread their prayer carpets on the ground, turn toward Mecca, and perform the prescribed rites. Women take no part in these rituals.

While farming is the main occupation of the village, there is some herding, too, especially for the agha and the few farmers who own larger plots of land.

Certain handicrafts must be performed even in the smallest villages. The work of carpenter, potter, weaver, shoemaker, laundryman, or barber is very important. The people who do these chores are known as *kammis*. For some of them, it is a part-time occupation; they also have small plots of land. Most of these services are paid for in food. The barber, for instance, cuts the hair of the entire family and gets a certain amount of food per year in return.

GETTING MARRIED

Strange as it may seem to the Western world, in a traditional family of Pakistan or Bangladesh man and wife may see each other for the first time only *after* they are married. The selection of a marriage partner is made by the parents or other next of kin.

In India, where the caste system is part of the religion, many people still will not marry below their own castes. But Pakistan and Bangladesh have no caste system, since all people are to be considered equal. While there are no castes, however, there are class groupings, or *baradar* — classes based on heredity, wealth, and occupation. For instance, the son of a lawyer would not think of marrying a peasant girl. There is no law against it, but it just isn't done. Social status is important. Most people marry within their class groups.

The highest social group consists of those who claim to be descended from Muhammad — the number is amazingly large — or from one of the many invading armies of long ago — Mogul, Tatar, Turkic, or Afghan, for instance. These people are called *ashraf* — "high-born." Strangely, the *ajlaf* — "low-born" — are those who cannot prove that their ancestors came into the country in comparatively recent times ("recent" in terms of a very ancient land). European newcomers also have high status, especially the children of mixed marriages with the British. Anxious parents keep the family trees very much in mind.

People get married young, mostly in their teens, and in Bangladesh younger than in Pakistan. After much searching, the proper mate is found. But complications do not end there. The bride price, called *mahr,* has to be agreed upon. It is paid by the family of the groom, preceded by much haggling, which, strangely, is sometimes in reverse. So as to gain "face" and to be talked about in town, a rich family wants to pay a high price.

Well-to-do families like to have a sumptuous wedding. People who can afford to spend money are admired. Actually, this is not much different from wedding customs in the United States, where the father of the bride is admired for footing the bill for a lavish wedding. The wedding itself is a great social occasion, especially in smaller places, and people may talk about it for years.

Wedding customs differ according to the families' means and in various parts of the countries. Even the poorer people want to show off, and often they run into debt. Many people are critical of this practice.

There are many wedding customs. One of them is that of the "seven wives," happily married women who sew the bridal gown to ensure happiness for the young couple. Another custom is tinting the bride's nails a reddish-orange, and giving her a tinseled red veil for the wedding. Red is, evidently, the color of luck. During the tinting procedure, the bride is expected to sing traditional songs. They express the hope that she will be able to keep her husband under control.

Finally, the day of the wedding arrives. The bride is garbed in traditional garments — *sahra,* a veil, and *gharara,* pajamalike pants. Her hair is decorated with flowers.

In the distance are heard the strains of music announcing the approach of the groom. He rides a horse and carries rich presents — if his family is wealthy. He brings a collection of many-colored saris and expensive jewelry.

Meanwhile, the wedding party has assembled in the village hall, led by a scholar learned in the Koran, the Sacred Book, and a lawyer. The bride and groom await them in separate rooms. The scholar reads passages from the Book, while the lawyer asks the groom, "Are you ready to wed your bride?" Of course, he says yes. Then the lawyer visits the room of the heavily veiled bride, asking the question. She says yes, and the marriage contract is completed. The young people remain in their separate rooms. They still have not seen each other. The marriage ceremony continues the following day.

On the next day the bride wears a red dress decorated with jewels, and she stays in her room. Her face is veiled. She stares at the ground as her husband is brought in. He wears a turban with a long fringe, which keeps him from seeing his wife. He bows his head to make sure that he doesn't look at her. They kneel on the floor, still looking down. But between them is a mirror. For the first time, they are able to see each other. The husband then says, "Wife, I am your slave."

But the wedding festivities are far from over. Now the newly married couple must visit their relatives. In certain sections, they receive sweetmeats on these visits. It is customary to give them 101 jars, symbolizing the hope that they will have 100 sons and one daughter. Sons are at a high premium in Muslim countries.

Such long weddings as this are costly. Some families spend their life savings on them. But there is a developing trend in modern Pakistan and Bangladesh to do away with these expensive ceremonies.

GOING TO SCHOOL

Only two out of ten people in both countries today know how to read and write. Even this is an improvement over the past. Education has been badly neglected, as it often is in tradition-centered Muslim countries. In some areas boys have been schooled only to recite the verses of the Koran. That was supposed to be enough education for a lifetime: the Koran was said to contain all the wisdom of the world.

But times are changing, and so is the attitude of both governments toward education. According to the governments, more than 8 million students are now in elementary schools, with over 3 million in secondary schools. Universities enroll about a half a million for both countries. After two years of college the student receives a bachelor's degree, and after another two years he receives a master's degree. This is in contrast to universities in the United States, in which four years are usually required for a bachelor's degree, and an additional two years for a master's.

Pakistan and Bangladesh have problems with education, as do many underdeveloped nations. When they were part of India, the British held the best jobs — in government, the military, law, and others. Now that the colonial officials are gone, almost all of the educated people want the best jobs. But a developing country needs educated people for technical work, too. Yet the young man or woman who has just received a college diploma does not want such work.

There is also the problem of language instruction. Bangladesh speaks Bengali, with many dialects. Pakistan speaks some thirty languages. It has tried to solve its problem by introducing Urdu, a mixture of several languages based on Hindustani. But it will take a long time before millions of people learn Urdu.

Although Bengali and Urdu are the national languages, the official business language of both countries continues to be English.

(67)

Right: kindergarten class
for Pakistani boys and girls.
Left: smoking the hookah.

FROM VILLAGE TO CITY

If a young man or woman from a village such as Punjabpur were to look for work in a larger town, he or she would find much that was familiar and much that was different.

A city such as Dherwarabad, for instance, with a population of about 50,000, has mud walls, courtyards, women's quarters, and wells in some sections. But it also has a noisy and picturesque bazaar where radios broadcast long passages from the Koran all day long. It also has movie theaters and restaurants.

Food is far more varied in Dherwarabad than in a small village. Famous, as well as delicious, are *kabobs,* small pieces of meat, seasoned and broiled, often with tomatoes, peppers, onions, and other vegetables, usually on a skewer. One of the varieties is prawn kabob. The prawn is a shrimp which, in the area's tropical waters, may reach two feet in length.

At its best, food in both countries is heavily spiced, often with curry powder. Curried chicken and lamb are popular, as are hot fried pastries filled with fiery spiced meat or peppery potatoes, called *samosas.*

Not many forms of art are found in cities of either nation, or anywhere in the countryside. Muhammad warned his people to stay clear of "carven images." But the love of art is expressed in architecture, especially in the mosques and tombs.

Music is very popular. The people enjoy the *narh,* a small reed instrument, and the *alhohoza,* a double flute. The *surando* is a string instrument that the player holds on his knees.

A visitor to the city will enjoy the *dara,* "guest house," in the home of a well-to-do citizen. There people sit on low divans along the walls. The dara has a *hookah,* also known as *nargile.* It is used for smoking tobacco, which is cooled as it is drawn through water with the aid of a long flexible tube. Each guest takes a few puffs and passes it on to his neighbor. Because of its more colorful life, the city has an increasingly powerful attraction for rural youth.

CHAPTER EIGHT
THE SCENE TODAY

Pakistan and Bangladesh are part of both the Middle East and the Far East. The USSR and Communist China are close neighbors; so are the countries of Southeast Asia. But Pakistan's main problem in international relations comes from a closer source — its continuing strife with India.

A major source of trouble between these two countries since the 1947 partition has been, and continues to be, the beautiful region known as Kashmir.

Before partition, Kashmir was the largest of the Indian princely states, with a territory of some 84,471 square miles. Its population was about 4 million. Three fourths of the people were Muslims. However, the ruler of Kashmir, Maharaja Hari Singh, was a Hindu.

The policy at the time of partition was to allow the princely states to decide whether or not to join either the Islamic Republic or India or whether to become independent countries. Hari Singh chose independence.

However, that was not the choice of some Muslims in the surrounding area. They declared a *jihad* — holy war — and swept into Kashmir, bent on forcing it to become part of the Islamic Republic. Most of the Muslims in Kashmir were sympathetic to the idea.

Singh, on the other hand, was not. He appealed to India for help. Indian troops entered Kashmir and pushed the Republic's invaders back into the mountains. India occupied and has held the most fertile part of the region, the Vale of Kashmir, with a population of more than 3¹/₂ million. The Islamic Republic established an Azad (Free) Kashmir government, with the capital at Muzaffarabad, in the rest of the country.

The dispute was brought before the United Nations. The Republic demanded that Kashmir should vote on which country to join. The government was confident that the Muslim majority would vote to join it. But India protested, declaring that at the time of partition the Maharaja had spoken for Kashmir. The situation has remained a stalemate, and through the years India has been governing most of Kashmir from its own capital of New Delhi. Even though India appointed a native Muslim as head of state in early 1975, Kashmir has remained a part of India; the Kashmir problem has not been solved.

The situation is still the same today and is the source of bad feeling between the two neighboring countries. Bound together by geography and history, Pakistan and India have grown far apart; for years transportation and trade between the countries were almost at a standstill. However, since 1974 commerce has increased. Both Pakistan and India spend large amounts on arms, money that could be far better spent for their own progress in other areas.

The Islamic Republic tried to strengthen its position by joining the Central Treaty Organization (CENTO) and the Southeast Asia Treaty Organization (SEATO). While still a member of both groups, Pakistan is not active in either one. The government has decided that a neutral position in world affairs is the wisest policy for the nation.

India and the Islamic Republic were approaching the edge of war in connection with an event that began peacefully enough. It was a national election in the Muslim nation that was to turn the country into a constitutional republic. The sequence of events began in 1970.

A constitution was to be framed, President Yahya declared. To do that a National Assembly (Congress) was to be elected by the people. The elections began on December 7, 1970. Because of the difficulty in reaching polling stations in some parts of the deserts, the elections lasted for ten days.

The most important political party in what was East Pakistan (now Bangladesh) was the Awami League, headed by a picturesque figure, Sheik Mujibur Rahman, a favorite of the people and a brilliant speaker. His platform was self-government for the east, so that it would not be oppressed by the west. In the west wing, the Pakistan People's Party was the most important contender, headed by Zulfikar Ali Bhutto, a well-known political figure. His party platform called for "Islamic socialism," in which a handful of rich families would cease to exploit the poor.

The election results stunned the country. The Awami League in the east made a clean sweep, getting nearly all of the assembly seats. Since the east has a majority of the population, the league would, therefore, have the majority in the assembly. In the west, Bhutto's party came out ahead of all others.

The attention of the nation now focused on the sheik. He had stated his terms before the election, and now he restated them. The eastern section was no longer to be treated by the west wing as a colony. It was to govern itself in all internal affairs. The federal government, however, was to deal with the entire country's defense, foreign affairs, and national currency. This was precisely the change that the west opposed.

Promptly, President Yahya flew to the eastern capital, Dacca, to persuade the sheik to change his stand — which Yahya considered extreme and would mean the breaking up of the country. The sheik stood his ground. Yahya decided to act — and act he did, leading to one of the greatest tragedies on the subcontinent. On March 25, 1971, he called the army into action, manned mainly by soldiers from the west wing. They occupied the eastern part, and were prepared to crush the Awami League. The sheik was spirited out of the east wing, jailed in the west, and charged with high treason. The National Assembly was called off.

A reign of terror began in the east wing. Suspected Awami sympathizers were slaughtered. Entire villages were reduced to ashes. The

massacre became indiscriminate. Additional targets of the occupying army were Hindus in the east. Some of the enraged easterners slashed back, slaughtering the western soldiers. How many people were killed in this senseless massacre nobody knows for sure. The estimated number of victims is a quarter of a million, including men and women of all ages.

Fear seized the villagers, especially the Hindus, and a tragic trek began. Some 9 million wretched people left their shacks and crossed the frontier into India. There they were placed in makeshift refugee camps, with inadequate care. Others made their homes in the woods, along the roads, in the gutters. Epidemics hit, including cholera. Thousands of children died of malnutrition, and tens of thousands were facing death. Adults died, too, in large numbers. Help came from abroad, but it was simply not enough.

In the eastern section, meanwhile, some of the people slashed back even more fiercely. They called for an independent country — Bangladesh — with no links to the Islamic Republic. President Yahya charged that India was fostering this movement, which he denounced as treason. He also made the claim that law and order were restored in the east. People were wondering how long order would prevail.

"The world watches the frontiers of India and Pakistan with increasing anxiety," the British foreign minister later told the United Nations. "There could be no greater tragedy for the world if India and Pakistan find themselves unwillingly at war."

But that tragedy did occur in late 1971, when fighting broke out in the eastern wing. India, with superior military power, sided with those who called for the creation of Bangladesh. The western forces were defeated, and the eastern wing declared itself to be an independent country.

As a result, Yahya Khan was forced to give up power. Zulfikar Ali Bhutto became Pakistan's first civilian president since 1958. In January, 1972, he placed the former president under house arrest, and released Sheik Mujibur Rahman from prison. The sheik — known as Mujib — returned to Bangladesh to lead his country.

In 1973 Pakistan agreed to release 175,000 Bengalis from Pakistan in exchange for non-Bengalis then in Bangladesh. Pakistanis adopted a new constitution in April of that year, making the country a federal Islamic republic with the executive power in the hands of a prime minister. Ali Bhutto became prime minister on August 15.

As the prime minister of Pakistan after the secession of the east wing, Zulfikar Ali Bhutto revealed impressive administrative skills and sensitivity to the people's needs. He started an ambitious economic program, based upon Pakistan's most vital industry: agriculture. He announced a land reform for the benefit of the peasants laboring on the rich people's farms.

Under Bhutto's leadership, conditions in Pakistan have been greatly improved. Compared to the former east wing, now Bangladesh, the country has one great advantage: it is not overcrowded. Though nearly six times the size of Bangladesh, it has a smaller population. Pakistan faces other problems, though. In some of its provinces there are movements to follow the example of Bangladesh and secede. Whether these movements will amount to anything only time will tell.

In contrast to Pakistan, Bangladesh is tremendously overcrowded, with a population of 75 million on a mere 55,000 square miles. It is one of the most densely populated countries in the world. Although it is a lush, green country, it is constantly exposed to awesome tidal waves and killing storms.

The "founding father" of Bangladesh is Mujibur Rahman, whom his people call Mujib. In his early youth he was already a rebel opposing the rule of Pakistan in his native East Bengal. Mujib was imprisoned several times. Between his spells in jail he served as the secretary of the Awami League, which called for the autonomy of the east wing. Then came the terrible uprising and the no less horrible suppression. In the end, Bangladesh became independent, and Mujib became prime minister in April, 1972. A constitution was framed, which became effective in December, 1972, and provided for a parliamentary government. The Awami League swept into power after the first elections in March, 1973. Mujib maintains strict control over the league.

While the former west wing had an auspicious start, Bangladesh has been sinking deeper into the mire of poverty. Today, an independent nation, it is worse off than it was as a part of Pakistan. It is afflicted with many of the plagues of underdevelopment. Its leadership has not been able to raise living standards. The government is often corrupt and inefficient. Disease and starvation are rampant. Bangladesh has become the poorhouse of Asia.

That is largely the situation today — the two former wings of the Islamic Republic of Pakistan are two independent countries, who must not only solve the many problems of their peoples but must also learn to get along with each other.

FOR FURTHER READING

Other related topics that may be of interest to the readers of this book are:

Bothwell, Jean. *The First Book of India,* rev. ed. New York: Watts, 1971.

Lengyel, Emil. *Iran.* New York: Watts, 1972.

———. *Modern Egypt.* New York: Watts, 1973.

———. *The Oil Countries of the Middle East.* New York: Watts, 1973.

Liversidge, Douglas. *The British Empire and Commonwealth of Nations.* New York: Watts, 1971.

Warren, Ruth. *The First Book of the Arab World.* New York: Watts, 1963.

INDEX

History of Indian subcontinent, 28–48

Holy wars. *See* Hinduism

Ibrahim Lodi, 31

India, 5, 7, 70, 71
    and British Empire, 2, 12, 28–48
    history, 2, 28–48
    independence, 2
    population, 1
    religion. *See* Hinduism
    social life, 2
    war with Pakistan, 1, 5

Indian Civil Service. *See* History of Indian subcontinent

Indian National Congress. *See* History of Indian subcontinent

Indus River, 7, 8, 17, 29

Industry
    Bangladesh, 27
    Pakistan, 8, 16

Iran, 5

Iraq, 29

Islam, 1–3, 11, 23, 28, 30, 49–55, 70, 71
    See also History of Indian subcontinent; Mosques

Islamabad, 11

Jahan, 8, 34

Jahangir, 8, 34

Jamuna River, 23

Jhelum River, 7, 48

Jihads. See Hinduism

Jinnah, Mohammed Ali, 39, 41, 43

Jute production, 27

K2, 5

Karachi, 8, 15, 16, 17, 20, 42

Karakorum Range, 12

Karnafuli River, 20, 30

Kashmir, 5, 7, 70, 71
    dispute between India and Pakistan, 1, 5

Khan, Liaquat Ali, 43

Khulna, 23

Khyber Pass, 12

Koran. *See* Islam

Lahore, 8, 11, 30, 49

Lake Rawal, 11

Little Calcutta. *See* Dacca

Mahmud of Ghazni, 30

Maliks. *See* Pathans

Manghla Dam, 48

Marriage customs, 64–67

Meghna River, 23, 24

Mogul Dynasty, 31

Mosques, 8, 11, 23, 49

Mound of the Dead, 28

Mountains, 5, 7

Muhammad. *See* Islam

Muhammad-al-Qazim, 30

Muhammad Iqbal, 38, 39

ABOUT THE AUTHOR

Born and educated in Budapest, Hungary, where he attended the University of Budapest, Emil Lengyel now lives in New York City. He was a prisoner of war in Siberia during World War I, and he lectured in American army camps during World War II. Mr. Lengyel has been a newspaper correspondent in Vienna and the United States, as well as a professor of history at New York University until 1960, when he joined Fairleigh Dickinson University in Rutherford, New Jersey. The author has written numerous adult books, and a number of children's books for Franklin Watts.